Why Do Cats Purr?

By Joy Radle Cutrone
Illustrated by Sharon Smith Lapham

Animal Humanity Books
Portland, Maine, USA

Published by Animal Humanity Books

Printed in the United States of America

Library of Congress Cataloguing-in-Publication Data
Cutrone, Joy Radle
Why Do Cats Purr?/by Joy Radle Cutrone;
illustrated by Sharon Smith Lapham

Summary: Learn what a cat needs to be happy.

ISBN 0-9727585-0-X

For Haley Jo and Tyler
...who teach me every day,
why do children laugh and sing?

Animal Humanity Books
Portland, Maine

Hi! I'm Ginger Kitty!
I live in a house on the edge of the city.
My favorite place is curled up in your lap.
Will you come join me in an afternoon nap?

Let's cuddle together
– oh do stroke my fur –
And I'll tell you my secret
Why cats like to purr.

The first thing to do
Is to keep us well fed
With moist cat food, dry cat chow,
And fresh water, it's said.

Do you think that's a start?
Try patting my head.
Do you hear that soft purr
From a satisfied cat?

**Tip: Always give a cat room to eat. Never crowd or take food
from an animal eating.**

I like to pounce and surprise you
And play ball on the floor.
When you hug me gently,
I respect you much more.

I'll grow old before you do,
So just keep in mind:
I like soft touches best -
Most loving, and kind.

Now what do you suppose
We cats like next best?
You guessed right again!
A nice place to rest.

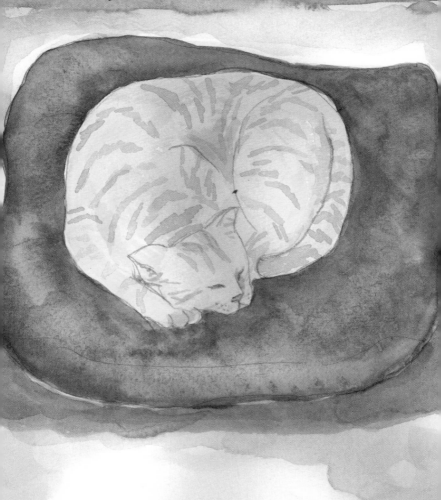

A soft pillow, a chair,
Or a sill does just fine -
In from the cold weather
A warm place to call 'mine.'

Tip: Domestic cats are safest living indoors, where they're not exposed to disease, harsh weather, or predators.

I'm a proud creature, you know.
I like to stay clean
With fresh litter, trim nails;
My coat brushed to a sheen.

I purr deep in my throat
- You've noticed, I bet -
When you bring me back home
From my check at the vet.

Tip: Clean cat litter every day. Babies, and pregnant and nursing mommies, should never handle used cat litter.

And last, but not least,
Yes, most important of all -
Is to know that you love me,
Winter, spring, summer and fall.

I know life brings changes
So I'll give you your space;
Just don't forget about me -
Let me, too, have my place!

**Tip: Cats like a place that's set away from activity,
or up off the floor, where they can sleep safely, and
keep an eye on what's happening around them.**

So if you let me love you
In my own feline way
My heart will grow fonder,
And my love will not stray.

Though I may not show it
My purr will tell all:
I may not be big
But my heart is not small.

So now you've learned,
I'm certainly sure,
That it's when cats are HAPPY
They are likely to purr!

Tip: Cats can be wonderful family pets. Just remember: never approach an animal you do not know without the assistance of an adult or permission from their owner.

If you would like to adopt a cat, promote humane education, or help a cat in need, the following resources are available:

The American Society for Prevention of Cruelty to Animals (ASPCA). Find your local chapter, an animal awaiting adoption, and vital information by visiting http://www.aspca.org, or by calling 212-876-7700.

The Humane Society of the United States (HSUS). Your local Humane Society shelter is a wonderful place to get a pet – as well as the education you need to properly care for your new friend and introduce him or her to your home. Find out how you can help promote the humane protection of all animals at http://www.hsus.org.

Petfinder. Find an animal available for adoption in your area at http://www.petfinder.com.

Please visit us at www.animalhumanity.org
Or write or call us at:
Animal Humanity Books, LLC
PO Box 3753
Portland, ME 04104
USA
Telephone 207-929-3858
Facsimile 207-929-3896
Email info@animalhumanity.org